ASH

GITA

ASHTAVAKRA

GITA

Translated by

HARI PRASAD SHASTRI

SHANTI SADAN
LONDON

First Edition 1949
Second Edition 1961

Reprinted
1972, 1978, 1984, 1992, 2009

© English Translation 2009
Shanti Sadan, London

www.shantisadan.org

ISBN 978-0-85424-028-9

SHANTI SADAN
Centre of Adhyatma Yoga
29 Chepstow Villas, London W11 3DR

*Printed and bound by
The Cromwell Press Group, Trowbridge, Wiltshire*

Dedicated to

UTTAMA DEVI

INTRODUCTION

THE word "Gita" means a song. There are many Gitas, of which some of the most beautiful appear in the classics Yoga Vasishtha and Shrimad Bhagavata. The Bhagavad Gita, which is incorporated in the Mahabharata, is held by the great Rishis to be unsurpassed.

The Ashtavakra Gita, less well-known in the West, expresses the highest teachings of the Upanishads, and embodies the philosophic thought of the Sages Yajnavalkya and Vamadeva. It does not give an exposition of the truth by logical reasoning, but a description of the bliss experienced by an illumined Saint.

Those who have not understood the essence of Vedanta and are still practising the discipline of self-purification, will probably not fully appreciate this work, but for the advanced student, the spiritual truth is here revealed in a simple, uncompromising form.

Each verse is a text for meditation; the whole work has a magic of its own, which elevates and exalts the mind and grants glimpses of the transcendental region.

INTRODUCTION

The particular school of Advaita Vedanta propounded in this Gita, is called Ajatavada, that is, the theory that the universe was never created in the Absolute. It is the most metaphysical explanation of the world, God and the Absolute.

It is by feeling and by saturating the mind in the great ideas so lyrically expressed in this poem that an aspirant attains an intuitive vision of the truth. This is the sure path to release.

The translator found this Gita a favourite text among the Mahatmas of the Himalayan regions.

CHAPTER I

1. Janaka said :

O Lord, tell me this : how does a man acquire knowledge of Truth, and how liberation, and how the practice of renunciation ?

Note : " Knowledge of Truth " means a knowledge of the nature of the ultimate Reality, which is the real Self of man.

" Liberation " means freedom from the influence of the conditioning principle called nescience, which is composed of the three gunas or modes :—Sattva, rajas and tamas—equilibrium, motion and inertia. This nescience is the root of all suffering.

2. Ashtavakra said:

O Friend! If thy aim in life is liberation then shun sense objects as poison, and pursue as nectar, forgiveness, simplicity of life, compassion, contentment and truth.

Note : " Sense objects " are passing, and the good in them is a characteristic of the all-pervading Truth ; devotion to them impoverishes the resources of the soul and becomes a binding factor. The word " truth " in this verse means truth-speaking.

1

3. Thou art neither earth, water, fire, air, nor ether. Know thy Self (Atman) as Witness of all these, and different from them, if thou would'st attain liberation.

Note : This verse provides a text for meditation. If done with feeling, bondage which is illusory like self-induced hypnosis, can be terminated.

4. If, detaching thyself from thy sense of identity with the body, thou remain at rest in Intelligence, thine will be spontaneous bliss, eternal peace and liberation from the imagined bondage.

5. Thou (as Atman) art not of the Brahmin or other castes, neither dost thou belong to any of the four stages of life. Thou art not an object of sense perception, thou art the Witness alone, unattached by nature and without form. Be blissful!

Note : " The four stages of life "—Brahmacharya (student life), Grihasthya (householder's life), Vanaprastha (forest life) and Sannyasa (life of renunciation).

6. O all-pervading Reality ! virtue and vice, pleasure and pain are modes of the mind, and thy Self is independent of them. Thou art neither the doer nor the enjoyer ; ever free art thou.

Note : This is an important verse. Our whole empirical life consists of streams of mental consciousness. Being above the mind, Atman is ever-free and all-bliss.

7. Thou art the one subject of all and in fact ever free. The cause of thy imagined bondage is that thou attributest subjectivity to objects rather than to the Self.

Note : In the highest sense, the Self is above the subject-object relationship, but in a relative sense it is called the subject to differentiate it from inert matter. The confusion between the real subject and the object creates bondage.

8. Egoism in the form of " I am the doer " resembles a great black and poisonous serpent. The antidote to its poison is recognition of the fact " I am not the doer." This knowledge leads to happiness.

Note : " Egoism "—the sense of narrow individuality, is called a black snake because it leads to forgetfulness of the nature of the Self. The conviction " I am not the doer " is the certain antidote.

9. The dark forest of ignorance (of the nature of Self) is the cause of grief and should be consumed by the conviction " I am the one ever-pure Consciousness."

Note : " Forest ". This word is well chosen. As a forest hides the objects in it, so ignorance obscures the vision of Truth.

10. Thou art that Consciousness, the supreme Bliss, in which the world appears as an imagined object, like a snake in a rope. Be happy ! That thou art !

3

11. He who thinks himself to be free, is free, and he who thinks himself to be bound, is bound. True is the saying, " as a man thinks, so he becomes."

12. The Self is the witness, all-pervading, perfect, free, one, consciousness, actionless, not attached to any object, desireless, ever-tranquil. It appears through illusion as the world.

Note : For the purpose of meditation, the attributes of the Self, which are really all negative, are spoken of as positive in this verse. For example, " perfection " here means absence of all want.

13. Always contemplate the ever-fixed Intelligence, the non-dual Atman. Giving up all inner and outer identification of the Self with the not-self, abandon the notion of the individualised self.

14. O Child, the net of self identification with the body has held thee imprisoned long enough. With the sword of the knowledge " I am Intelligence " cut this illusion and be blissful.

15. Thou art wholly independent, actionless, self-luminous and without fault. Thy bondage is that thou deemest thyself to be liberated through the practice of Samadhi.

Note : The practice of Samadhi is contingent on the hypothetical bondage. When the truth is known there is no need of Samadhi.

16. The Universe is pervaded by thee and exists in thee. Verily by nature thou art Consciousness Absolute ; do not harbour narrowness of heart and think thyself to be otherwise.

17. Free art thou from modifications ; independent, calm, without dimension or form, imperturbable, thy nature unimaginable Intelligence. Know thyself to be pure Consciousness.

18. Know all that has form to be unreal, and the formless to be the Self. By means of this knowledge thou shalt avoid the possibility of rebirth.

19. Within and without the form reflected in the mirror, exists the mirror. Likewise the Supreme Lord exists within and without the body.

Note : The meaning is that the form in the mirror has no real existence; its appearance is phenomenal. The body and the mind similarly have no real existence; by superimposition they seem to exist. The mirror symbolizes the Self, and the body and mind in no way influence it.

20. As the jar is pervaded inside and outside by the same ether, so does the all-pervasive Reality (Brahman) abide in all things.

CHAPTER II

1. Janaka said:

How wonderful! I am tranquil, taintless, pure Knowledge, transcending matter (Prakriti). Until now, I have been deceived by illusion.

2. As I, by my light, reveal this body, so do I reveal the whole Universe. To me it belongs, or it is nought.

Note.—The dream either belongs to the dreamer, or it is nothing.

3. Through renunciation of this great Universe together with the body, I now perceive the supreme Self, by the skill of my Yoga.

4. As waves, foam and bubbles are not different from water, so in the light of true knowledge, the Universe, born of the Self, is not different from the Self.

5. As a piece of cloth is found, on reflection, not to be different from its threads, so this Universe, on reflection, is found not to be different from the Self.

6. As the juice of sugar cane wholly pervades the sugar produced from it, so the Universe, produced phenomenally in me, is pervaded by my Self.

7. The world appears as a result of ignorance of the nature of the Self, and it disappears when the nature of the Self is recognised. The illusory snake is born of the absence of knowledge of the rope, and it disappears when knowledge of the rope is attained.

8. My nature is Knowledge and nothing other than Knowledge. Verily the Universe is revealed under the light of my Self.

9. How strange that the world has its appearance in me, due to nescience, like the illusory silver in the mother-of-pearl, the snake in the rope and the mirage in the rays of the sun.

10. From me the world is born, in me it exists, in me it dissolves ; as jars return to clay, waves to water and bracelets to gold.

11. Wonderful am I, my salutations to my Self ! I am beyond the range of decay. When the whole world from Brahma to a blade of grass is destroyed, I still remain.

12. Wonderful am I ! In spite of the body and its properties, I am one. I go nowhere, I come from nowhere, I abide in my Self, pervading the whole Universe.

13. All praise be to me, I am most skilful, I, without a form, uphold the Universe through all eternity.

14. I am wonderful, adoration to my Self. I own nothing, and yet all that is thought or spoken of is mine.

Note : As Atman (the Self) possesses nothing, yet the whole phenomenal Universe belongs to the noumenon.

15. In reality, Knowledge, the Knowable and the Knower do not exist in me. That faultless Self am I, by whose want of Knowledge the three appear to exist.

16. The conception of duality is the root of all suffering ; its only cure is the perception of the un-reality of all objects and the realisation of myself as One, pure Intelligence and Bliss.

17. I am pure Intelligence ; through ignorance I have imagined the illusory conditions in myself ; meditating thus, all the time, I am the Absolute.

Note : The word " Upadhi " translated here as " conditions " means Maya, the illusory principle which causes the Self to appear as the world.

Some authors call Upadhi a medium through which the Self manifests itself, but strictly speaking, it is not so.

8

18. I am neither bound nor free. My illusion has ended. The world, though appearing to exist in me, has in reality no existence.

Note : When the illusion of duality has vanished, still the world seems to appear, but the Gnani knowing it to be unreal is not affected by it.

19. My conviction is that the Universe and the body have no reality. The Self is nought but Intelligence; how can the world be imagined in it ?

20. I am the Self, and my nature is pure Consciousness. The body, heaven, hell, bondage, freedom and fear are merely imagined, and I have no relationship with them.

Note : If the body and the world are taken as real, then the Self cannot be held to be real, being radically different in nature from them.

A is A, and B is B—A cannot be B, and vice versa.

21. I see no duality. Why should I become attached to a multitude of human beings who resemble a wilderness to me?

Note : Although apparently there may be a multitude of human beings, the illumined Sage is only conscious of the One.

22. I am not the body and the body does not belong to me. I am pure Intelligence. My only bondage was my desire to continue to live as a cognitive entity.

9

23. I am the limitless ocean in which, on the rising of the wind of the mind, the worlds are produced, as waves on the sea.

24. When the wind of the mind has died away in the ocean of my Being, then the ship of the universe perishes, together with its trader, the jiva.

25. How strange that in me, the limitless ocean, the individualised selves, arise as waves. They cross each other, play for a while, and disappear, according to their respective natures.

Note : Avidya (nescience) and Karma are responsible for the Universe.

CHAPTER III

Ashtavakra said :—

1. Knowing the Self to be indestructible and one by nature, how is it that thou, having attained wisdom, art still concerned with the acquisition of wealth ?

2. A craving for the objects of the senses rises out of the illusion caused by ignorance of the real nature of the Self ; just as the illusion of silver in the mother-of-pearl causes an attachment for it.

3. Why should one who knows his Self to be That in which universes rise and fall like waves in the sea, run hither and thither like a suffering creature?

4. Having heard that his Self is pure Consciousness, and of surpassing attraction, why is he still attached to lust which gives rise to increased body consciousness?

5. How strange that the Sage who knows all beings to be in the Self, and the Self to be in all beings, should still continue to harbour the sense of possession.

6. It is strange that one who is established in the great truth of non-duality, and is desirous of liberation, should allow himself to be weakened by the practice of amorous pastimes.

7. Lust is radically opposed to knowledge. How strange that one who is physically enfeebled and has reached the end of his life, is still eager for sensual enjoyment.

8. How strange that he who is indifferent to the objects of this world and the next, who discriminates between the eternal and the passing, and who yearns for emancipation, should still fear the loss of individuality, occasioned by release.

9. The wise man who is serene within, ever perceives the absolute Self, and is neither pleased nor angry when abused and tormented.

10. The Mahatma regards the actions of his body as not different from those of another body. Whether praised or blamed, he abides in the Self, undisturbed.

11. He who has realised the Universe as mere phenomenon, and has lost all real interest therein, does not fear the approach of death.

12. He whose mind is desireless even in disappointment, and who is fully satisfied with the knowledge of the Self, he is verily incomparable.

13. Knowing the objects of perception to be nought by nature, that steady-minded one neither accepts this, nor rejects that.

14. Having given up all attachment to external objects and transcended the influence of the pairs of opposites, the Sage, free from desire, does not feel pleasure or pain in anything he experiences.

CHAPTER IV

Ashtavakra said:—

1. The wise man who has known the truth about the Self plays the game of life, and there is no similarity between his way of living, and the deluded who live in the world as mere beasts of burden.

2. The Gnani does not feel elated even in the supreme state which Indra and all other gods ardently desire and suffer through not obtaining.

3. The knower of truth is not affected by vice and virtue, as the sky is not really affected by the smoke with which it is covered, though it appears to be.

4. The knower of truth, the great-souled one, who has known the Universe to be nothing but his own Self, lives as he pleases.

Note : The " great-souled one " though free from all moral injunctions and prohibitions, lives strictly according to Dharma, which becomes part of his nature. His delusion having been destroyed, he goes beyond evil, and is not attached to good.

5. Of the four kinds of created beings from Brahma to a tuft of grass, the wise alone, renouncing desire and aversion, know all to be Brahman.

6.   Indeed, how rare is the great-souled one who has realised the Self to be the One without a second, and also the personal God. He does what he considers to be worth doing; he is without any fear whatsoever.

CHAPTER V

Ashtavakra said:—

1.   Thou hast no association with anything; pure art thou. What is there to renounce? Destroy the identity with the body and the mind, and enter into the state of the noumenon.

2.   As bubbles arise in the ocean, so does the universe arise in the Self. Thus knowing the Self to be all, enter into the state of the noumenon.

3.   Though the universe is perceptible by the senses, yet it has no factual existence, like the snake in the rope. Therefore, enter into the state of the noumenon.

4.   Be equable in pleasure and in pain, in hope and despair, in life and in death. Thus enter into the state of the noumenon.

CHAPTER VI

Ashtavakra said:—

1. I am infinite like space, the phenomenal world is like a jar. This is true cognition. The world has neither to be renounced, accepted, nor negated.

> Note : In this chapter, the holy Sage exposes the highest aspect of Truth. The world is a mere picture, drawn by illusion on the Self. To renounce or accept it, is to attribute reality to it.

2. I am like the Ocean in which the worlds are the waves. This is true knowledge, and renunciation, achievement or negation have no place in it.

3. I am like mother-of-pearl, and the imagined world is like the illusory silver in it. This is true knowledge which does not admit of renunciation, achievement or negation.

4. I am in all beings, and all beings abide in me. This is true knowledge which does not admit of renunciation, achievement or negation.

CHAPTER VII

Janaka said:—

1. In me who am like an infinite sea, the boat of the world is driven here and there by the wind of its own nature. I remain unaffected.

2. I am the boundless sea, let the waves of the world rise and fall in it. I am neither increased nor diminished thereby.

3. In me, the infinite ocean, arises the imagined universe. Tranquil and attributeless, my Self abides for ever.

4. The infinite and ever pure Atman is not in the object, nor is the object in it; free from attachment and desire, ever tranquil, in this Truth I abide.

5. Indeed, I am Consciousness Absolute, and the world is a magic show. The thought of acceptance and rejection does not exist in me.

CHAPTER VIII

Ashtavakra said:—

1.   It is bondage when the mind desires anything, when it grieves over anything, when it accepts, rejects or feels joy or anger in relation to anything whatsoever.

2   It is release when the mind neither desires nor grieves, is neither angry nor joyful, neither accepts nor rejects anything.

3.   It is bondage when the mind is attached to any sense perception; it is liberation when it is not so attached.

4.   Where there is " I " there is bondage, where there is no " I " there is release.   Know this to be the truth, and neither reject nor accept anything.

Note :   Passions trouble the mind, and worldly associations disturb it.   When it is in a state of tranquillity, it reflects the Spirit.

CHAPTER IX

Ashtavakra said:—

1. Duties discharged and undischarged or the pairs of opposites, when do these cease, and for whom? Realising this, cultivate inner renunciation and passionlessness.

> Note : " Realising " here means realising the unreality of the world, the sense of duty and also the pairs of opposites.

2. O My Child! That blessed one is indeed rare who has extinguished the passion for life, enjoyment and even learning, by observing the ways of men.

3. The wise become tranquil on realising that all objects of the world are subject to the threefold misery, that they are transient and of no actual (positive) reality, and should be rejected at all times.

> Note : " Three-fold misery " means those that pertain to the mind, those that are caused by animate and inanimate objects, and those that are caused by cosmic forces like floods, earth-quakes and so forth.

4. There is no time and no age in which men are free from the pairs of opposites. He who disre-gards them, content with whatever comes, obtains perfection.

5. What man is there, who, having observed the diversity of opinion among the great Sages, Saints and Yogis, does not become indifferent to learning and attain peace?

6. He is a true spiritual Guide who has obtained knowledge of the nature of Reality through indifference to the world, equanimity and reasoning, and who is animated by a desire to enlighten others.

7. In the modifications of the elements, see nothing but matter itself; thus attain freedom from bondage, and rest in thine own nature.

8. Renounce desire through inherent detachment; renounce the objects of the world, and renunciation of desire will follow. Thereafter live wherever thou pleasest.

CHAPTER X

Ashtavakra said:—

1.   Give up the chief enemy, desire for pleasure and for worldly prosperity, both being fraught with evil, as well as enslavement to Dharma (good deeds) from which they spring.

> Note : The three objects of the worldly-minded are Kama (pleasure), Artha (prosperity), and Dharma (good deeds), but release from the bonds of nescience should be the ultimate purpose of life.   Truth cannot be discerned unless Kama, Artha and Dharma are transcended.   This is the step beyond virtue and Plato's " Ultimate ".   Knowledge and not benevolence produces the state of complete freedom.

2.   Look upon friends, possessions, wealth, mansions, wives, gifts and other good fortune as a dream or a magic show, lasting only three or five days.

3.   Know that where desires prevail, there is the world.   Cherishing feelings of steadfast non-attachment, free thyself from desire and be happy.

4.   Desire constitutes the only bondage; to be freed from it is liberation.   By cultivating indifference to worldly objects, one obtains the bliss of realisation.

5.   Thou art One, pure Consciousness.   The world is inert and unreal.   Even ignorance is non-existent. Therefore, what desire can'st thou cherish?

6.   In countless former births thou wast attached to land, sons, wives, joys, bodies and pleasures, and yet they have ended.

7.   Bring to an end wealth, desires, and good and pious deeds, they will not bring rest to thy mind in the gloomy forest of the world.

8.   How many incarnations hast thou devoted to the actions of body, mind and speech? They have brought thee nothing but pain, why not cease from them?

CHAPTER XI

Ashtavakra said:—

1. One who has finally learnt that it is in the nature of objects to come into existence, to change and finally to pass away, he easily finds rest through detachment, and is freed from suffering.

2. Being convinced that Ishwara is the Creator of all, and none other, one should remain serene and unattached to any object.

3. He is ever content who is convinced that adversity and prosperity come in the fullness of time or are caused by Karma. His senses are controlled, he neither desires nor grieves.

4. Knowing for certain that joy and suffering, birth and death, are the result of Karma, he realises that it is not possible to accomplish desires; he sits tranquil, and though engaged in actions, is not affected by them.

5. Anxiety produces misery and nothing else. He who realises this relinquishes all desires and is calm and happy.

24

6. "I am not the body, nor is the body mine. I am Intelligence itself." He who has attained this knowledge has reached the state of the Absolute and ceases to think on what he has done, and what he has not done.

7. "Verily all is my own Self, from Brahma to a blade of grass." This conviction brings freedom from desire and imagination, and gives purity and serenity. Reasoning thus, a man does not concern himself with what has been attained or what is to be attained.

8. He who is convinced that this manifold and wonderful Universe has no real existence, becomes free from desire, is pure Intelligence, and finds peace in the knowledge that nothing is real.

CHAPTER XII

Janaka said:—

1. First I relinquished physical action, then immoderate speech and thought; now I abide in peace.

2. Having relinquished all attachment to sound and other objects of sense, and also the Self, as Self is beyond perception (and conception), I now remain at peace, my mind being freed from agitation and distraction.

3. Concentration is needed when the mind is distracted by false identification; realising this, I abide in peace.

4. O Sage! I am not concerned with what is to be accepted and what rejected. I experience neither joy nor sorrow. Thus do I abide.

5. I am as indifferent to the presence of the four stages of life as I am to their absence. Meditation, and renunciation of the contents of my mind, are likewise not for me. This is the state in which I abide.

6. Both performance and cessation of action are notions born of nescience; knowing this, thus do I abide.

7.   To attempt to think of the Self which is beyond the range of thought is only to create a new thought. Abandoning such a thought, I abide in peace.

8.   Blessed is he who is established in this peace; such a man has realised his own nature.

CHAPTER XIII

Janaka said:—

1.   Even a monk possessing nothing, does not easily find that tranquillity which is inherent in one who is free from desire for action.   I have renounced both action and renunciation of action, and live happily in any state.

2.   Renouncing identification with the body the tongue and the mind, I have acquired that state which is above desire, fatigue and ferment.   Therefore, I abide in happiness.

3.   Realising that the Self is actionless, I do whatever presents itself, and live happily.

4.   Action or inaction is for those attached to the body.   Having neither association nor dissociation with it, I live in perpetual bliss.

5.   Neither good nor evil results for me from activity, rest or sleep.   Therefore, I am happy whether at rest, active or asleep.

6.   Neither do I lose nor gain by sleeping or striving—giving up all thoughts of loss and triumph, I live happily.

7.   The varying aspects of pleasure are subject to change, under different conditions.   I am happy because I have gone beyond good and evil.

CHAPTER XIV

Janaka said:—

1. He who has acquired vacuity of the heart, who thinks of objects only by chance, who appears as if awake though really asleep, has verily expunged all impressions and experiences of worldly objects from his mind.

2. My desire to live and enjoy having died out, of what use to me are wealth, friends, learning, philosophy, and those thieves, the sense objects?

3. Having known the supreme Self, the Witness, and the Lord, my desire for liberation and my fear of bondage have left me.

4. The states of mind of that man whose doubts have ended, but who acts outwardly like one still in ignorance, are only understood by those who resemble him.

CHAPTER XV

Ashtavakra said:—

1. The pure-hearted man fulfils the supreme purpose of life through the instructions of his Guru, even though they be casually imparted. The worldly-minded man studies and enquires throughout his life, yet remains unenlightened.

2. A distaste for the objects of sense is liberation; attachment to those objects is bondage. This is wisdom; now act as thou wilt.

3. Knowledge of the imperishable Essence makes a worldly, active and eloquent man inactive, silent and wise. What wonder that the holy Truth is shunned by those still attached to the pleasures of the world!

4. Thou art not the body, nor does the body belong to thee, nor art thou the doer nor the enjoyer. Thou art Intelligence Itself, ever the Witness and free art thou! Live in bliss!

5. Desire and aversion are attributes of the mind; the mind does not belong to thee. Free from scheming and doubting, know thyself to be the immutable Intelligence and live in bliss.

6. Knowing that thy Self is the Self of all beings and that all beings abide in the Self, released from egoity and the sense of mine and thine, live in bliss.

7. Thou art that Intelligence in which the worlds rise like waves in the sea; be freed from the fever of duality, and live in bliss.

8. Have faith, O Darling, be not deluded! Thou art the Lord of the Universe; thou art Knowledge itself; thou transcendest Nature; verily thou art the Self.

9. The body is moved by the Gunas; it comes, stays and goes. The Self neither comes nor goes; there is no cause for grief.

10. Let the body last until the end of the world-period, or perish today; nothing can be added to or subtracted from thy Self, which is pure Knowledge.

11. In thy Self, the infinite ocean, the universes rise and fall of their own accord like waves. Let them rise or fall; they do not touch thee.

12. My Child, thou art pure Intelligence, the world is not distinct from thee; therefore the thought of rejecting or accepting anything is meaningless.

13. How can there be birth, action or even the sense of individuality in thee who art ever tranquil, and by nature pure Intelligence?

14. In whatever is manifest, thou alone appearest. Bracelets, armlets and rings made of gold are not other than gold.

15. Renounce all sense of distinction, such as " I am he ", " I am not this ". Know all to be thine own Self, and free from desires, be happy.

16. The world is the result of ignorance of thine own nature; in reality thou alone art. There is neither jiva nor Ishwara, nothing other than thyself.

17. He who has fully realised that the universe is a pure illusion, becomes desireless and Consciousness Itself—such a one abides in peace.

18. In the ocean of the world, One alone was, is, and will be. There is neither bondage nor liberation in thee. Live in perfect happiness, and in the consciousness that all is achieved.

19. Do not disturb thy mind with acquiring or relinquishing anything. Abide in the bliss of thine own nature.

20. Give up meditation; hold nothing in thy mind. Thou art free, and Bliss Itself; what wilt thou accomplish by thought?

CHAPTER XVI

Ashtavakra said:—

1. My Child, study and discussion of different philosophies will not establish thee in the Self. Forget all, and be happy.

2. O Wise One! Thou may'st take delight in action or in contemplation, but thy mind will still yearn for That which is beyond all objects and in which all desires are extinguished.

3. All are afflicted by reason of their exertions. Alas! this is understood by none; but he who is wise achieves emancipation through this very teaching.

4. That master idler to whom the opening or closing of the eyes is an infliction, to him belongs real bliss and to no other.

5. When the mind is free from ' this I have done and this remains to be done,' it transcends the desire for religious merit, worldly prosperity, sensual enjoyment and also liberation.

6. He who disdains sense objects is unattached, he who craves for sense pleasures suffers attachment; but he who neither rejects nor accepts is neither attached nor unattached.

7.   The notion of desire and aversion is born of lack of true discrimination.   The root and branch of the tree of phenomenal existence is dependent on these two.

8.   Activity begets attachment, renunciation gives birth to aversion; but the wise man lives like a child, free from the pairs of opposites.

9.   One who is attached to the world, desires to renounce it in order to avoid suffering, but the Sage who has no attachment, does not suffer even in the world.

10.   He who has a feeling of ' I-ness ' even for release, and retains his body-consciousness, is neither a wise man nor a spiritual aspirant; his lot is suffering.

11.   Even though Shiva, Vishnu or Brahma instruct thee, unless thou regardest the world as unreal, and dismissest all sense of egoity, thou wilt not become established in thine own nature (the Self).

CHAPTER XVII

Ashtavakra said:—

1. He who is always contented, who is unattached to any object, who ever enjoys solitude, he has obtained the fruit of spiritual Knowledge and of the practice of Yoga.

2. The knower of Truth does not suffer either inwardly or outwardly, for he knows that he alone fills the universe.

3. No sense object ever pleases him who delights in the Self, even as the elephant who delights in Sallaki leaves is not pleased with the leaves of the Nima tree.

4. Rare indeed is the Sage who does not crave for that which he has enjoyed, and has no desire for that which he has not possessed.

5. In the world those who crave for mundane joys and those who crave for liberation are found, but rare is that great-souled one who cares neither for enjoyment nor liberation.

6. It is only an enlightened man who has no attachment to righteousness, prosperity, sense delights or even liberation, and is indifferent to life and death.

7. Neither does the existence nor the dissolution of the universe cause him either delight or aversion. That blissful Sage lives happily on whatever comes.

8. He who has this spiritual Knowledge, whose mind is absorbed in contemplation and who is contented, lives in bliss whether seeing, hearing, touching, smelling, or eating.

9. Attachment and detachment are the same to him for whom the ocean of the world has disappeared. His gaze is withdrawn (from external objects), his actions are without motive, his senses are inoperative.

10. He who is freed from the mind neither sleeps nor wakes, neither opens nor closes his eyes, but enjoys the supreme bliss under all conditions.

11. The liberated man is ever rooted in his own nature, and is pure in heart, free from all desires under all conditions.

12. Seeing, hearing, touching, smelling, eating, acquiring, speaking and walking, the great-souled one, above action and inaction, is verily liberated.

13. The great-souled one neither commends nor censures anyone, he is neither angry, nor does he rejoice; he neither gives nor receives; he is free from attachment to objects.

14. Whether he perceives a woman full of love or death approaching him, the great-souled one remains unperturbed, rooted in his own nature. Verily he has found liberation.

15. The serene Sage recognises homogeneity everywhere, and perceives no difference in pleasure or pain, man or woman, prosperity or adversity.

16. For the man who is no longer bound by ignorance, the cause of birth and death, there is neither a desire to inflict injury nor to demonstrate compassion. He experiences neither arrogance nor humility, wonder nor agitation.

17. The liberated man has no aversion for sense-objects, nor does he crave for them. With his mind ever detached, he is unconcerned with what is attained and with what remains unattained.

18. The wise man who has acquired mental vacuity (the mind being filled with Atman alone), is not concerned with contemplation or its absence. He is established in the Absolute State, and has transcended good and evil.

19.   Devoid of the feeling of " This is mine " and
" This I am " and knowing for certain that nothing
objective exists in reality, the knower of Truth is at
peace within himself, his desires having subsided.
Though appearing to act, in fact he does not engage
in action.

20.   His mind having ceased to function and being
free from delusion and inertia, the man of Self-
knowledge experiences the indescribable state.

CHAPTER XVIII

Ashtavakra said:—

1. Salutations to That which is bliss, peace and light, with the dawning of the knowledge of which, all delusion as to the phenomenal Universe passes away like a dream.

Note : " Light " is here used in the sense of " Pure Consciousness."

2. Having acquired much wealth, one enjoys countless worldly pleasures, but to know true happiness one must renounce them.

Note : The insecurity of worldly enjoyments is summed up by the poet Bhartrihari in the following words :—" In enjoyment there is the fear of disease ; in social position the fear of loss of status ; in wealth the fear of hostile kings ; in honour the fear of humiliation ; in power the fear of foemen ; in beauty the fear of old age ; in scriptural erudition, the fear of opponents ; in virtue the fear of traducers ; in the body the fear of death.
" All the things of the world, pertaining to men are attended by fear ; renunciation alone, eliminates all fear."

3. He whose heart is parched by the sun of affliction arising from the sense of duty, experiences no happiness until his mind has acquired tranquillity.

4. The Universe is merely a mode of the mind; in reality it has no existence. Those liberated beings are surely immortal who are identified with Reality —which is self-luminous, and which needs no support for Its existence, but which cognises both existence and non-existence.

5. The nature of the Self is absolute, immutable, taintless. It is not distant, nor is it subject to attainment (being ever attained). This is Truth.

6. In those who have cognised the Self, illusion is dispelled, and the light of pure Consciousness shines through them; their distress is at an end and they live in bliss.

7. The wise know that all that is not the Self is merely a movement of the mind; being liberated, they live as a child lives.

8. Having finally realised that the Self is Brahman, and that existence and non-existence are imagined, what should such a one, free from desires, know, say or do?

> Note : The knowledge of the Self as Brahman reveals the unreality of all that is not the Self. No one who knows the river in a mirage to be an illusion, desires to bathe in it.

9. All such ideas as " this am I " and " this I am not " end in the conviction that all is the Self. Realising this, the Yogi becomes silent.

10. For the Yogi who has become inwardly calm there is no distraction, no concentration, no increase or decrease of knowledge, no joy and no grief.

11. The dominion of Heaven, or indigence, profit or loss, society or solitude, are the same to the Yogi who has realised his nature to be free from all conditions.

12. The Yogi who has transcended dualistic reasoning, such as ' this I have done, this still remains to be done,' sees no significance in ritual, material prosperity, sense enjoyment or discrimination.

13. The Yogi who is liberated while yet in life has no further duties to perform, nor is his heart attached to anything; his actions in this world are appearances only.

Note : The Yogi is internally free, but his Karma continues to operate ; he is not affected by such actions, being beyond the idea of body or Karma.

14. The Yogi who has passed beyond the region of desires finds no significance in phenomena, in the universe, in contemplation on That, or in liberation.

15. He who sees reality in the universe may try to negate it. Not so the Mahatma who has rooted out all desires; not seeing, he appears to see.

16. He who has known Brahman meditates on " I am Brahman," what should he who sees no duality meditate upon?

Note : One who sees Brahman has not realised his identity with Brahman. The dual consciousness is there, making it possible for him to meditate on " I am Brahman."

When the highest state is reached, identity is established, and no such meditation is possible.

17. He who is conscious of distraction, practises self-control; the illumined sage, having nothing further to accomplish, has no need of self-discipline.

18. Though the man of spiritual knowledge appears to act like others, in fact he does not do so, for he sees no necessity for Samadhi, nor does he perceive distraction or any taint in his own essence.

19. Free from desire, he is neither conscious of existence nor non-existence (of the world) but is ever satisfied and wise; though appearing to act, nothing is done by him in reality.

20. He who experiences the supreme bliss of his own nature, and whose mind is ever tranquil and pure, he has no need to renounce, nor does he feel the lack of anything in himself.

21. The mind of the Sage does not give rise to the modifications of concentration, distraction or prejudice; his actions are not subject to any code, nor is he affected by honour or dishonour.

22. He who by right knowledge has transcended the world of appearance, for him there is neither joy nor sorrow. With a serene mind he lives as one unrelated to his body.

23. He whose delight is in the Self, and who is consequently serene and pure, has no desire to renounce anything, nor does he feel any lack anywhere.

24. He who has acquired the natural state of vacuity of mind may act as he pleases ; he is not affected by honour or dishonour as are ordinary men.

25. One who acts in conformity with such pure thoughts as ' the body is the actor and not the Self,' though appearing to act, does not act.

26. The liberated Sage acts apparently without motive or purpose and may be regarded as a fool, but in reality he has transcended action. Although appearing as happy and blessed in the world, verily he has gone beyond it.

27. The wise man, weary of reasoning, who has attained supreme peace, neither thinks nor knows, nor hears nor sees.

28.   That man of peace, beyond distraction and contemplation, is neither an aspirant for liberation, nor is he bound.   Knowing the universe to be an illusion, though perceiving it, he remains in the absolute state.

29.   He who still retains his egoism is mentally active even when at rest; but the wise man who is free from egoism is incapable of sin or wrong action.

30.   The mind of the freed Sage is unmoved by trouble or pleasure; it is inactive, static and desireless and also free from doubts.

Note : " Static " here implies that the jiva is detached from the vrittis of the mind and not identified with them.

31.   The mind of the Sage is free from effort whether meditating or acting.   His actions and meditations are not prompted by personal motives.

32.   An ignorant man is bewildered on hearing the spiritual Truth, but a wise man, on hearing the Truth, withdraws his consciousness within himself, even though he appears like a fool outwardly.

Note : The spiritual Truth does not reveal itself to an unpurified mind, and the aspirant must undergo a course of spiritual discipline before he can recognise it.

33. Those unaware of the Truth practise concentration and discipline, but the wise who have found the Infinite Atman within their own Self, are eversatisfied and recognise no further cause for action.

34. Whether he lives a life of action or withdraws from the world, the ignorant man does not find spiritual peace, whereas the Gnostic discovers the Truth and so becomes happy for ever.

35. Though relying on different practices, men do not recognise the Self which is Intelligence Itself, ever pure, beloved, perfect, transcending the changing universe and free from any conditions.

36. An ignorant man does not attain liberation though repeatedly practising concentration; whereas that blessed one through spiritual knowledge is ever free and devoid of all activity.

37. The ignorant man does not realise Brahman, because he still desires to know Him (implying that he is separate from Him). The wise man, however, realises the nature of the Supreme Brahman without desiring Him.

38. Without the foundation of real knowledge, the ignorant yearn for liberation but do not achieve it. The wise, having transcended ignorance by truth, sever the root of all misery.

45

39. There is no spiritual peace for the ignorant, because they desire and seek it in the external world; the wise realise it internally as ever achieved, and are at peace.

40. Where is Self-knowledge for him who depends on external things? Ignoring the world, the wise contemplate the Immutable Self.

41. The ignorant who strive for control of the mind never achieve it; but the wise, whose chief delight is in the Self, achieve it without effort.

42. Some recognise the existence of Being, and some deny it; rare is the one who bestows no attention on phenomena and enjoys peace.

43. Although those of little intelligence regard Atman as secondless and undifferentiated, yet being under the delusion of relativity, they fail to realise It, and are therefore subject to suffering as long as they live.

44. The intellect of one who longs for liberation is relatively dependent (namely on the triad: the Knower, the Known and Knowing), but the intellect of the liberated one is independent (the triad being dissolved in absolute Knowledge), and is free from desire.

45. Becoming aware of the tigers of sense-objects, bewildered souls, seeking a shelter, resort to the cave of contemplation for the acquisition of self-control.

46. Seeing the lion of desirelessness, the elephants of the sense-objects quietly depart, or remain to serve him like slaves.

Note : The meaning is that he who is desireless and un-attached to sense-objects subdues them completely.

47. He who has resolved his doubts and whose mind is absorbed in the Self, no longer seeks the means to liberation. Seeing, hearing, touching, smelling, eating, he lives happily in the world.

48. He who is self-controlled and whose intellect is pure, by the mere hearing of the truth, becomes indifferent to the enjoined rules of conduct.

49. Whatever is to be done he does without effort; like a child, his conduct is neither good nor evil.

50. Independence (of desire and aversion) is the means to liberation, happiness and peace. The supreme state of consciousness is also attained through independence.

51. All modifications of the mind are dissipated when a man realises that he is neither a doer nor an enjoyer.

52. The mind of the wise man, subject to no restraint and free from guile, shines forth in glory; whereas the fool whose mind is full of desire, simulates tranquillity.

53. Sometimes the wise of freed intellect, who have transcended the mind and are no longer bound, disport themselves in various pastimes, and sometimes they retire into deep mountain caves.

54. No desire rises in the heart of the wise on looking upon a venerable brahmin, held in reverence, or a god, or a sacred spot, or a woman, or a king, or a dearly loved one.

55. The Yogi remains tranquil and unperturbed even when despised by his servants, children, wives, grandchildren and other relatives.

56. Though he appears pleased, in fact he is not pleased; though he appears to suffer, yet he is not in pain. Only those who have realised the supreme condition will recognise his state.

57. A sense of duty is not recognised by the wise; for them the world is void, and their true Self is immutable and pure.

58. The unenlightened man, even when doing nothing, is agitated; whereas the enlightened Sage remains calm even while fulfilling worldly duties.

59. The man of calm intellect is happy in ordinary life, whether sleeping, acting, speaking, or eating.

60. He who in the realm of relativity, by virtue of his self-conquest, does not behave like an ordinary man, remains undisturbed like the calm surface of a vast lake, his sufferings at an end.

61. Even the passive and introspective life of a deluded man produces activity; whereas the life of action of the wise results in inactivity.

62. The deluded man often manifests aversion to his possessions, but he who has transcended attachment to the body is free from desire and aversion.

63. The deluded man is ever identified with thinking and not thinking, whereas the spiritual man has transcended both these principles.

64. The Sage, like a child, while seemingly engaged in action is perfectly detached; without a motive, he is not identified with the work in which he is apparently engaged.

65. Blessed is the Sage who has realised the nature of the Self and is the same in all conditions; who though acting in the world of relativity does not identify himself with it.

66. To the wise, ever peaceful and infinite like space, where is the reflected Self, where is the world, where the means and where the end?

67. Verily glorious is the Sage, free from all desires and the embodiment of infinite bliss; he has attained the natural state of Samadhi through realising the Unconditioned.

68. In brief, the great-souled knower of the ultimate Truth has no desire for enjoyment or liberation, and is freed from attraction at all times and in all places.

69. To the great Sage the whole Universe from Mahat (cosmic intellect) to the changing world, is nothing but a name. He who is pure and perfect and has withdrawn from all existence, to him nothing remains to be accomplished.

70. That enlightened one who has known with certainty that the world is nothing but the product of illusion and does not exist in reality, to whom the inexpressible is known, he enjoys natural peace and bliss.

71. To him for whom there is no objective reality and who is of the nature of pure Intelligence, what rules of conduct should he follow, what need of renunciation and restraint for him?

72. The Sage who has realised his own infinity and is not conscious of relative existence, is freed from bondage and liberation, joy and sorrow.

73. Before the state of self-realisation the world exists only as Maya. The Sage, living devoid of the feeling of " I " and " mine," is without attachment.

74. To the Sage who knows himself to be the universal Self, indestructible and free from suffering, what is knowledge, the universe and the feeling that " I am the body " and " the body is mine "?

75. As soon as an ignorant man relinquishes control over the mind and his spiritual practices, he becomes a prey to desires and fancies.

76. The foolish man, even after hearing the spiritual Truth, still clings to his delusion; he may through his efforts manifest tranquillity of mind, but in reality he still craves for the enjoyment of sense objects.

77.   He from whom activity has dropped away on the dawn of spiritual knowledge, finds no purpose in doing or saying anything, even though he appears to act in the eyes of others.

78.   For the knower of Truth, who is ever fearless and immutable, there is neither darkness nor light, nor renunciation, nor anything whatsoever.

79.   What is fearlessness, discrimination or stability to the Yogi who is indescribable and impersonal by nature?

80.   For the Yogi there is neither heaven nor hell nor even liberation in life.

81.   The wise do not desire to achieve anything nor does lack of success cause them pain.   Verily their tranquil minds are ever filled with immortal bliss.

82.   The desireless man does not praise the forbearing, nor does he censure the evil-doers; equally content in happiness or misery, he finds no duty to be done.

83.   The wise do not look on birth and death with aversion, nor are they anxious to perceive the Self. Free from joy and grief, they transcend life and death.

84. Glorious are the wise who are free from desire for sense-objects, and from attachment to son, wife and other relationships. Free are they also from the care of the body.

85. The wise man is contented whatever comes to him; he wanders about at will, and rests wherever the sunset overtakes him.

86. The great-souled one, entirely dependent on the Self, is oblivious of the cycle of birth and death, and cares not whether his body is born or dies.

87. Blessed is the Yogi without attachment or possessions, who moves about at will, who is free from the pairs of opposites and whose doubts have been dissolved.

88. He is glorious who is devoid of ' my-ness,' to whom gold, earth, and stone are the same, who is neither influenced by rajas or tamas and the knots of whose heart are severed.

89. That liberated one is beyond comparison, within whose heart there is no desire, who is wholly unattached and ever contented.

90. The wise man, freed from all limitations, knows yet knows not, sees yet sees not, speaks yet speaks not.

91.   Whether he be a king or a beggar, he who is free from pleasure-desires is supreme; in his conviction there is neither good nor evil.

92.   To the Yogi who has fulfilled the supreme purpose of life, and who is the embodiment of simplicity and rectitude, what is licence and what is restraint, and what need for the determination of Truth?

93.   How can the inner experience of the one who is desireless, whose sufferings are at an end and who rests in the calm of the Self, be described?

94.   Contented under all conditions is the Yogi who sleeps not in the sleeping state, who dreams not in the dreaming state and who wakes not in the waking state.

95.   The man of knowledge is free from thought though appearing to think, is free from sense-organs though appearing to possess them, is free from intelligence though appearing to be endowed with it, and is without a sense of ego though appearing to possess it.

96.   He is neither happy nor unhappy, neither attached nor unattached, neither liberated nor desirous of liberation, he is neither this nor that.

97. The illumined one is not distracted even in a state of distraction, is not meditative even in meditation, is not dull even in a state of dullness, is not learned even though he appears to be possessed of learning.

98. The Self-realised and liberated Yogi, who under all conditions abides peacefully in the Self, who is free from all conceptions of duty and action, being desireless, never considers what he has done, and what he has not done.

99. He is neither pleased when praised, nor angry when blamed; he neither fears death, nor rejoices in life.

100. The enlightened one neither avoids the crowd, nor seeks the forest. Under any conditions, in any place, he remains unmoved.

CHAPTER XIX

Janaka said:—

1. From the inner recesses of my heart I have erased all shades of opinion through the instrumentality of the knowledge of Truth.

2 Abiding in my glory, I see neither Dharma, Kama nor Artha—discrimination, duality, nor non-duality.

Note : Dharma, Kama, Artha—righteousness, legitimate pleasures and material prosperity are the recognised fruits of good conduct. See note to X. 1 on page 22.

3. Abiding in my own glory, where is past, present, future, space, or eternity for me?

4. Abiding in the bliss of realisation, I have no consciousness either of Self or non-self, good or evil, hope or fear.

5. Free from the waking, dreaming and deep-sleep states, for me who abide in my own glory, even the fourth state does not exist; how can there then be fear?

Note : " The fourth state "—transcendental Bliss.

6. Established in the supreme state, where is distance, where proximity, where grossness, where subtlety, where the external, where the internal for me?

7.   Resting in my own effulgence, neither life nor death exist for me; for me there is no relativity nor worldly phenomena, no withdrawal, nor Samadhi.

Note : " Withdrawal "—Laya—meaning the lapse of the mind into sleep, instead of resting it on the Absolute. It is one of the obstacles to Samadhi.

8.   Reposing in my own Self, what need have I to dwell on the three ends of life, or on Yoga or on wisdom?

Note : " Three ends of life " Dharma, Artha and Kama.

CHAPTER XX

1.   In my perfect being (Atman) neither the elements, nor the body, nor the sense-organs, nor the thinking principle, nor the void, nor despondency exist.

2.   What need is there for desirelessness or contentment, or what meaning have the Scriptures, Self-knowledge and the mind and its objects to me, who am without a sense of duality?

3.   What is knowledge, what ignorance, what the limited ego, or " I ", " This ", or " Mine ", what is bondage or freedom to me, where the definition of the Self?

4.   What is prarabdha Karma, what is liberation in life, or liberation at the time of death to the undifferentiated?

Note : Prarabdha—means the Karma which fructifies in this life, and must be worked out before the death of the body.

5.   Where is the doer or the enjoyer, and where the rising or vanishing of thought? Where is direct perception of Reality for me who have cast off individuality?

6. For me who am free and above unity and multiplicity, there is no world and no candidate for release; neither do I recognise the state of contemplation nor the state of knowledge. The state of bondage and liberation are one to me.

7. Having realised my own nature, the undivided essence, the manifestation and withdrawal of the world no longer exists for me. Where is the goal, and where the purpose; where the seeker and where the liberated one?

8. Neither am I knowledge, the vehicle of knowledge, nor the object of knowledge. What is entity or non-entity to me who am eternal perfection?

9. What are joy and grief, distraction and concentration, dullness and delusion to me who am actionless?

10. Being freed from all mental activity, where is relativity, where transcendence, where joy and where grief for me?

11. Being ever perfect, neither Maya nor the world, neither attachment nor detachment, neither Jiva nor Brahman exist in me.

12. For me who am immutable, indivisible and rooted in the Self, there is neither the path of action, nor of renunciation, neither bondage nor release.

13. I am Shiva, the unconditioned, the absolute Good. What need is there for instruction or scriptural injunction? I am neither Guru nor disciple.

14. What need for further declarations? Nothing emanates from me, nor does existence or non-existence, unity or duality abide in me.

SHANTI SADAN PUBLICATIONS

AVADHUT GITA

❝Words cannot describe
this Consciousness Absolute.
The mind is lost in Its majesty.❞

The exalted verses of this famous Gita are ascribed to the Mahatma Dattatreya. They describe, in a simple and lucid style, the knowledge and bliss of an illumined sage.

'The Avadhut Gita is a special classic which is meant for the use of those advanced students of Indian metaphysics who have learnt self-control to an appreciable extent, risen above the prejudice of this or that religion, and made the ultimate Reality— Truth—their sole God.'

978-0-85424-002-9

3nd Edition, 3rd Imp.   40pp Paper